1000 WORDS NATURE

Jules Pottle

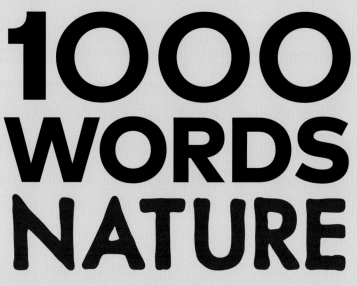

DK

DK | Penguin Random House

Written by Jules Pottle
Senior Editor Dawn Sirett
Designed by Rachael Hare, Karen Hood,
Samantha Richiardi, Sadie Thomas
DTP Designer Vijay Kandwal
Additional Editing Robin Moul
Design Assistance Sif Nørskov
Picture Researcher Sumita Khatwani
Jacket Coordinator Issy Walsh
Production Editor Abi Maxwell
Pre-production Manager Pankaj Sharma
Production Controller Isabell Schart
Managing Editor Penny Smith
Deputy Art Director Mabel Chan
Publishing Director Sarah Larter

First published in Great Britain in 2022 by
Dorling Kindersley Limited
DK, One Embassy Gardens, 8 Viaduct Gardens,
London, SW11 7BW

The authorised representative in the EEA is
Dorling Kindersley Verlag GmbH. Arnulfstr. 124,
80636 Munich, Germany

Copyright © 2022 Dorling Kindersley Limited
A Penguin Random House Company
10 9 8 7 6 5 4 3 2 1
001–326507–Jan/2022

A CIP catalogue record for this book
is available from the British Library.
ISBN: 978-0-2415-3338-3

Printed and bound in China

For the curious
www.dk.com

FSC
www.fsc.org
MIX
Paper from
responsible sources
FSC™ C018179

This book was made with Forest Stewardship
Council ™ certified paper – one small step in
DK's commitment to a sustainable future.
For more information go to
www.dk.com/our-green-pledge

1000 WORDS NATURE

A note for parents and carers

The importance of knowing about nature

In this technological age, being aware of the beauty and complexity of nature is an important part of our wellbeing. If you take the time to look and listen to what is around you, you'll discover all sorts of natural wonders. Even on a city street, the world is teaming with plant and animal life, and in every habitat on Earth, each living organism is important in its own way.

Young children are natural explorers. They like to touch and smell and immerse themselves in their environment. This book will give them the vocabulary to talk about what they have experienced, and build their knowledge of topics relating to wildlife, the environment, and our planet. It will prompt children to ask questions and lead them to look further and to learn more.

I grew up with "elephant" and "giraffe" as familiar words in my alphabet books, but my grandchildren may never see those animals in real life. We have reached an important moment in the future of our planet. The choices we make now will affect the lives of our children and our children's children, so it is important that we are all fully informed of our impact on the planet and what we can do to protect it. This book is a great place to start a young child's appreciation for the natural world and to begin to talk about living responsibly on our planet.

Jules Pottle
Primary science consultant, teacher, trainer, and author

Contents

SAFETY INFORMATION

Outdoor recreational activities are by their nature potentially hazardous. Parents need to assist and supervise their children for many of the nature activities shown in this book. Everyone should assume responsibility for their own actions and prepare for the unexpected for a safer and more enjoyable experience.

Our planet

Earth orbits the Sun in space. Inside Earth is a hot core of liquid rock. Around the outside of Earth there are gases, called Earth's atmosphere. Earth formed a very long time ago. Its landscape and wildlife have changed over time.

Earth

outer space

Is most of Earth's surface covered with land or with water?

Moon

land

Some landscape features

crater

volcano

mountain

valley

river

lake

geyser

spring

rock

North Pole

crust

mantle

meteor

outer core

inner core

ocean

atmosphere

South Pole

Sun

stars

Some animals from long ago

Megazostrodon

pterosaur

dinosaur

ichthyosaur

mammoth

Which animal from long ago has a name that means terrible lizard?

7

Our world's resources

Our world is filled with useful materials. We must try not to waste them. We also need to reduce the pollution that some materials cause.

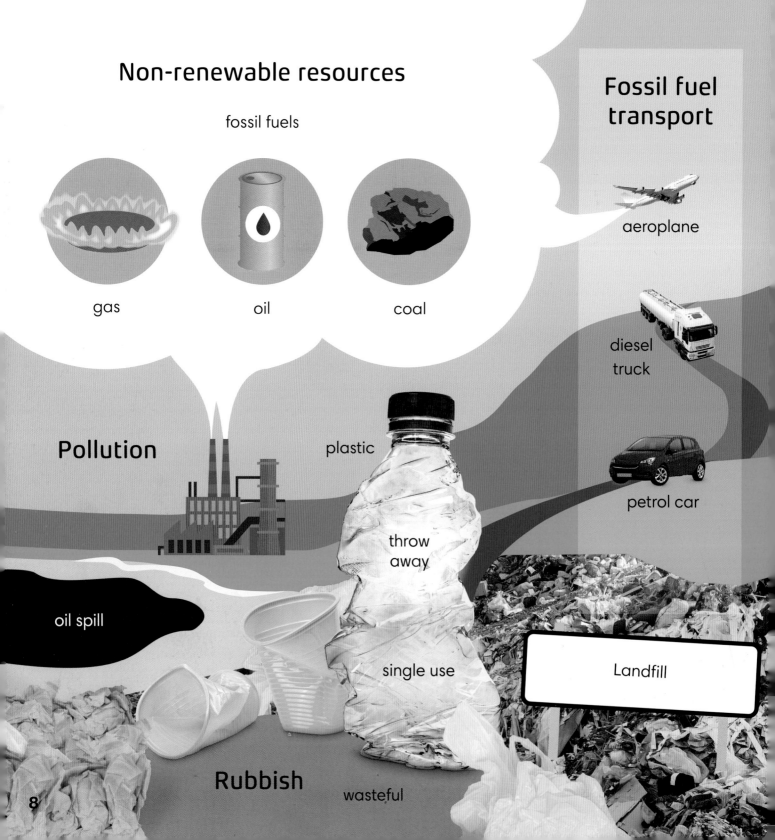

Non-renewable resources

fossil fuels

gas

oil

coal

Fossil fuel transport

aeroplane

diesel truck

petrol car

Pollution

plastic

throw away

oil spill

single use

Landfill

Rubbish

wasteful

8

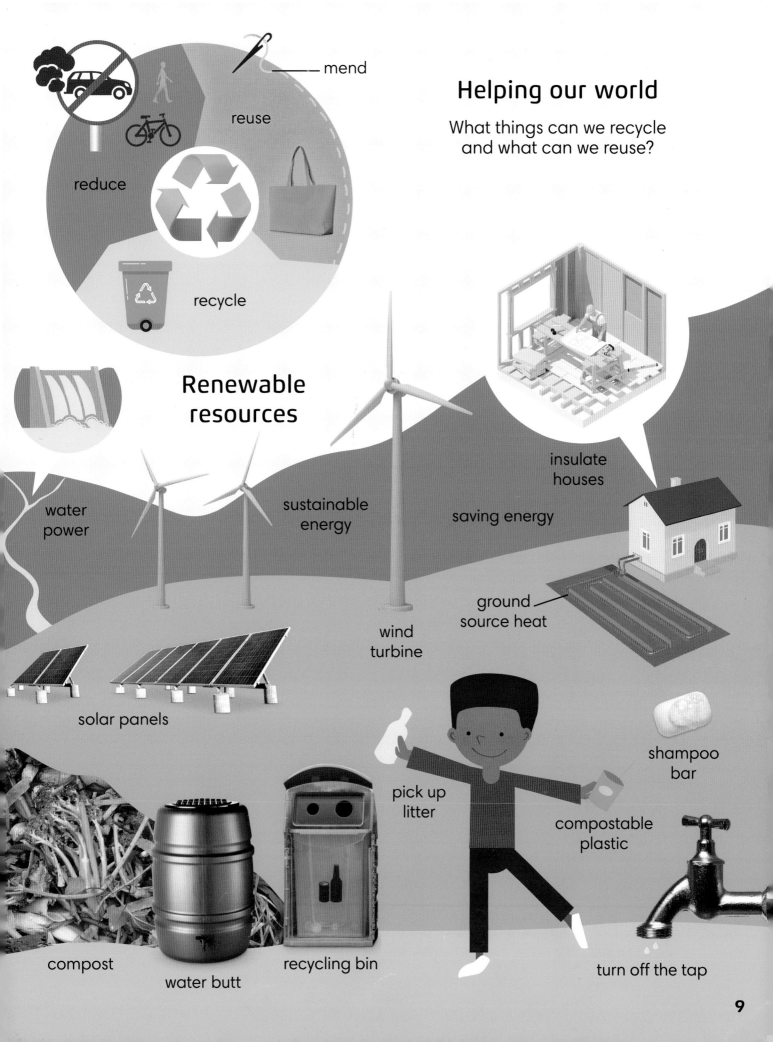

mend

reuse

reduce

recycle

Helping our world

What things can we recycle and what can we reuse?

Renewable resources

water power

sustainable energy

insulate houses

saving energy

ground source heat

wind turbine

solar panels

pick up litter

shampoo bar

compostable plastic

compost

water butt

recycling bin

turn off the tap

Humans and nature

For thousands of years, we humans have made nature work for us. We should do this respectfully, taking care of our planet and the things that live on it.

On the farm

fruit trees

tractor

wheat crop

fields

milking shed

cow

geese

goats

grain

fruit

sheep

chickens

vegetables

pigs

Have you ever taken care of a pet? What do pets need?

Pets

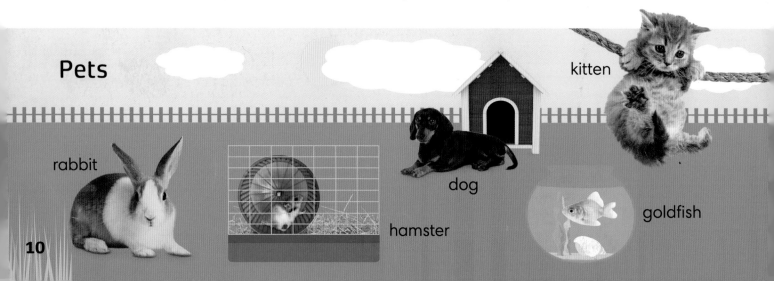

kitten

rabbit

dog

hamster

goldfish

fish farm

beekeeping

bees

honey

beehives

Unusual farm animals

ostriches

crocodiles

snails

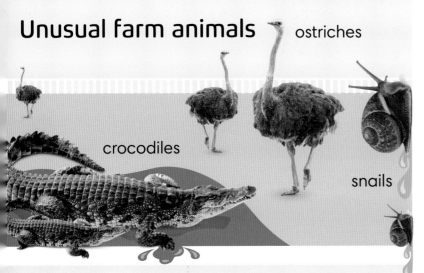

Working animals

sheepdog

guide dog

police horse

More types of farming

flower farming

rice farming

vineyard

tea plantation

Farms around the world grow different crops. Do you know what's grown in a vineyard and used to make wine?

Working with water

dam

canal

Mining

limestone quarry

coal mine

Nature activities

There are so many fun things we can do when we go out and enjoy nature.

nature spotting

bark rubbing

nature trail

binoculars

building a den

tree hugging

touching

splashing in puddles

pond dipping

net

nature art

collecting

fishing

Forest school

reading a map

We could start a nature collection. What things might we collect?

binning litter

12

paddling

flying a kite

building a sandcastle

crabbing

sledging

throwing snowballs

making a snow angel

snow person

Let's choose some things we'd like to do when we go out.

camping

storytelling

stargazing

night walk

treehouse

birdsong

listening

looking

bird watching

smelling flowers

digging

watering plants

picking apples

sweeping leaves

planting seeds

having a picnic

13

Weather

The weather is different in different places. Some countries have four seasons; others have two.

What's the weather like today?

Sunny

blue sky

sun hat

hot

sun cream

heatwave

Wet

rainbow

thunderstorm

drizzle

lightning

umbrella

fog

rain

puddles

Cold

icicles

hail

snowflakes

snowstorm

woolly hat

ice

snow

frozen

frost

14

Cloudy

overcast

cirrus clouds

stratus clouds

cumulus clouds

Windy

The water cycle

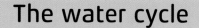

Clouds form (made of water drops).

Rain, snow, or hail falls.

Water vapour cools.

Water vapour forms.

Liquid water changes into gas.

Water (from rain, snow, or hail) flows into rivers and seas.

Four seasons

| spring | summer | autumn | winter |

Two seasons

dry season

wet season

What type of weather do you like best?

Extremes

From hurricanes and floods to dry deserts and frozen lands, our planet has some extreme weather and some incredible locations.

Spot a type of foggy weather that is caused by air pollution.

Extreme weather

drought   arid

flood

tsunami

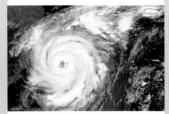

cyclone

hurricane

tornado

smog

sandstorm

extreme heat and wildfires

hailstorm

blizzard

ice storm   freezing

Incredible locations

Dead Sea, Asia

lowest land area on Earth

Mount Everest, Asia

highest land area on Earth

Furnace Creek, North America

hottest recorded temperature

Vostok Station, Antarctica

coldest recorded temperature

Atacama Desert, South America

driest place

Mawsynram, Asia

has highest rainfall

Angel Falls, South America

highest waterfall

Grand Canyon, North America

longest canyon

Kilauea Volcano, Oceania

Earth's most active volcano

Great Barrier Reef, Pacific Ocean

largest coral reef

Mariana Trench, Pacific Ocean

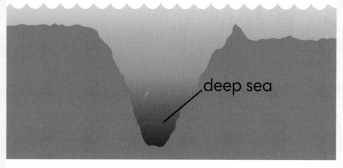

deep sea

deepest part of the ocean

Which of these amazing places would you like to explore?

17

Kingdoms of living things

Different features help scientists put all living things into groups. Here are the five major groups, called kingdoms, and some of the smaller groups that are within each kingdom.

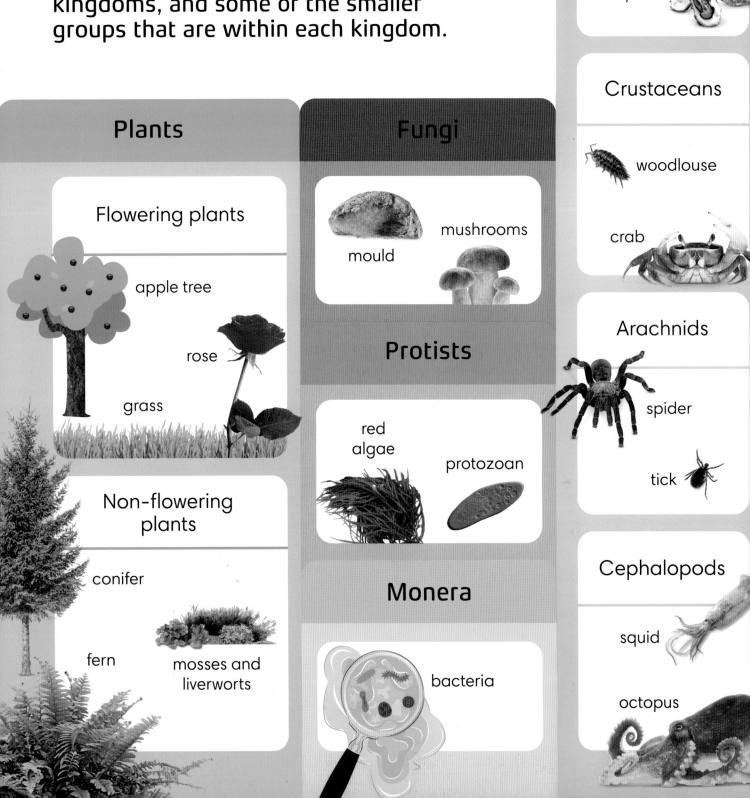

Plants

Flowering plants

apple tree

rose

grass

Non-flowering plants

conifer

fern

mosses and liverworts

Fungi

mould

mushrooms

Protists

red algae

protozoan

Monera

bacteria

Molluscs

snail

oysters

Crustaceans

woodlouse

crab

Arachnids

spider

tick

Cephalopods

squid

octopus

Animals

Echinoderms
starfish

sea urchin

Mammals
dolphin

kangaroo

human

Cnidarians
jellyfish

coral

Birds
robin

penguin

Reptiles
snake

crocodile

Amphibians
newt

frog

Poriferans
sponge

Let's think of some more mammals and some more reptiles.

Fish
clownfish

shark

Insects
ant

butterfly

Myriapods
millipede

centipede

Annelids
leech

earthworm

All sorts of plants

There are many different plants, but they all do something amazing – they use water, air, and sunlight to make their own food. This process is called photosynthesis.

Herbs can be used to flavour food. What herbs have you tried?

Shrubs

hydrangea

boxwood

Herbs

basil

thyme

Flowers

hibiscus

scent

petal

bud

orchid

leaf

stalk

thorn

daffodils

tulips

rose

Guess where baobab trees store water.

Weird plants

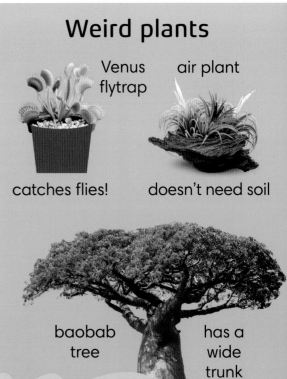

Venus flytrap

air plant

catches flies!

doesn't need soil

baobab tree

has a wide trunk

Climbers

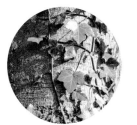

ivy

runner bean

Cacti

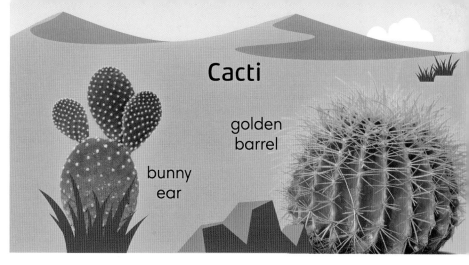

golden barrel

bunny ear

Trees

broadleaved

maple

weeping willow

palm

conifers

fir

pine

Fruit and vegetables we eat

orange

apple

kiwi fruit

carrots

cabbage

broccoli

Water plants

seaweed

water lily

Photosynthesis

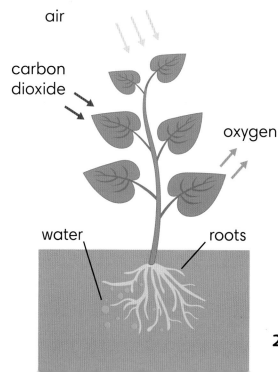

sunlight

air

carbon dioxide

oxygen

water

roots

21

A closer look at trees

A tree is a tall plant with a thick stem called a trunk. Like all plants, trees improve air quality by absorbing carbon dioxide and giving out oxygen.

sun

oxygen

Tree leaves

lobed

prickly

pointy

wavy edges

needles

pine needles

pine cone

twigs

Parts of a leaf

tip

vein

midrib

margin
(edge)

stem

roots

evergreen
keeps leaves all year

pine tree

carbon
dioxide

Tree flowers

cherry
blossom

hazel catkins

apricot buds

Tree fruits

apples

plums

lemons

oak
tree

branch

wood

tree rings

oak leaf

bark

tree
knot

trunk

sticks

acorns

deciduous
loses leaves
in autumn

The seed of an oak tree is inside an acorn.
Where would you find the seeds of a pine tree?

23

Plant and fungus life cycles

Most plants grow from seeds, bulbs, or tubers. Fungi grow from tiny spores.

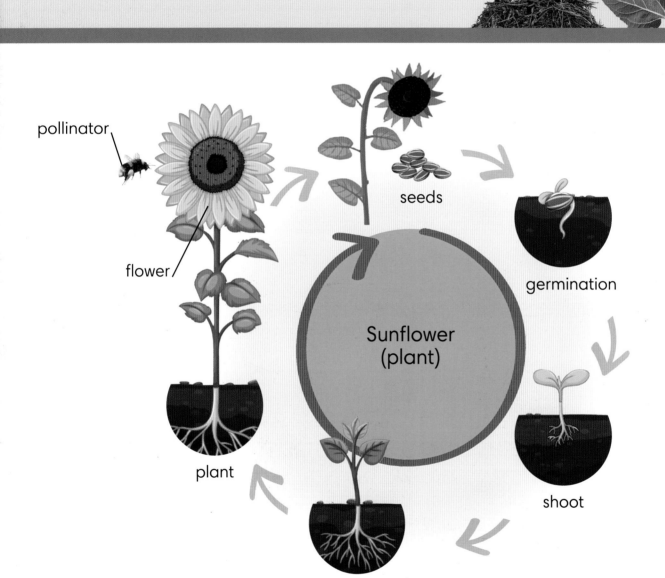

pollinator

flower

seeds

germination

Sunflower (plant)

shoot

plant

seedling

Have you planted any seeds? How did you take care of them?
Think of some things you did to help them grow.

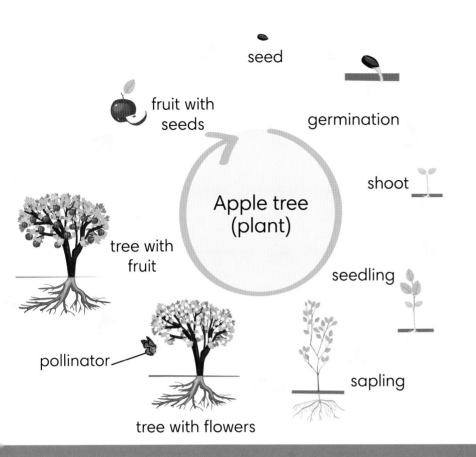

seed

germination

fruit with seeds

shoot

Apple tree (plant)

tree with fruit

seedling

pollinator

sapling

tree with flowers

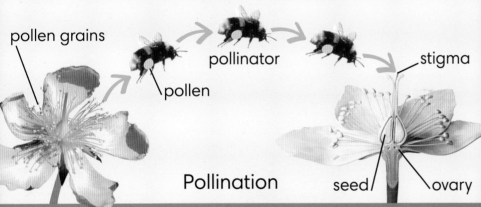

pollen grains

pollinator

pollen

stigma

seed

ovary

Pollination

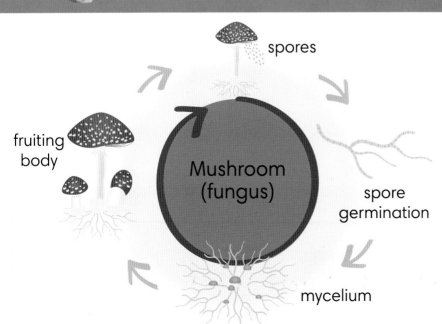

spores

fruiting body

Mushroom (fungus)

spore germination

mycelium

seeds in woody scales

pine cone

sycamore seeds

avocado stone

seeds (peas)

pea pods

Bulbs and tubers

tulip bulbs

potato tuber

25

Animal life cycles

Cats have kittens, and the kittens grow into cats. Then those cats have kittens. Let's learn more about animal life cycles.

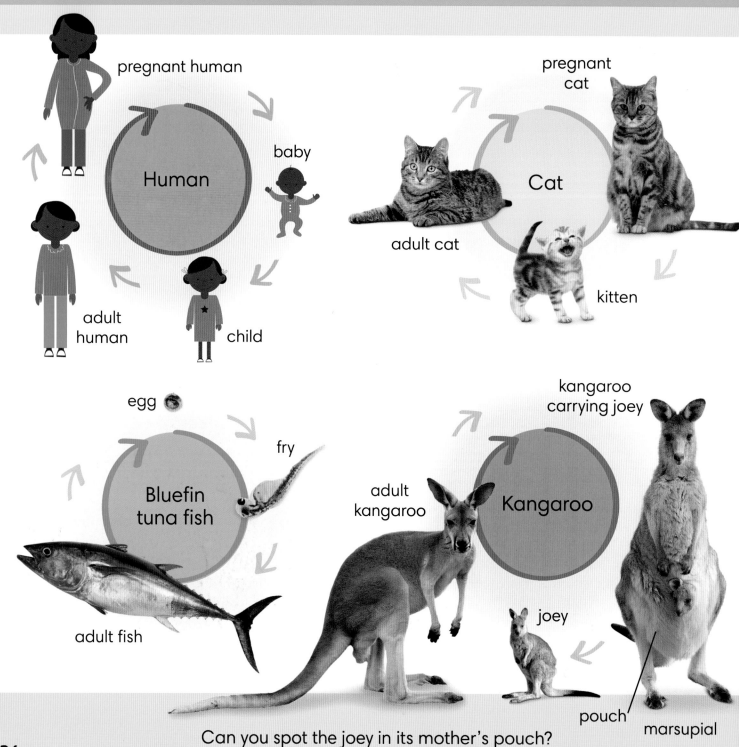

pregnant human

baby

Human

adult human

child

pregnant cat

adult cat

Cat

kitten

egg

fry

Bluefin tuna fish

adult fish

kangaroo carrying joey

adult kangaroo

Kangaroo

joey

pouch

marsupial

Can you spot the joey in its mother's pouch?

26

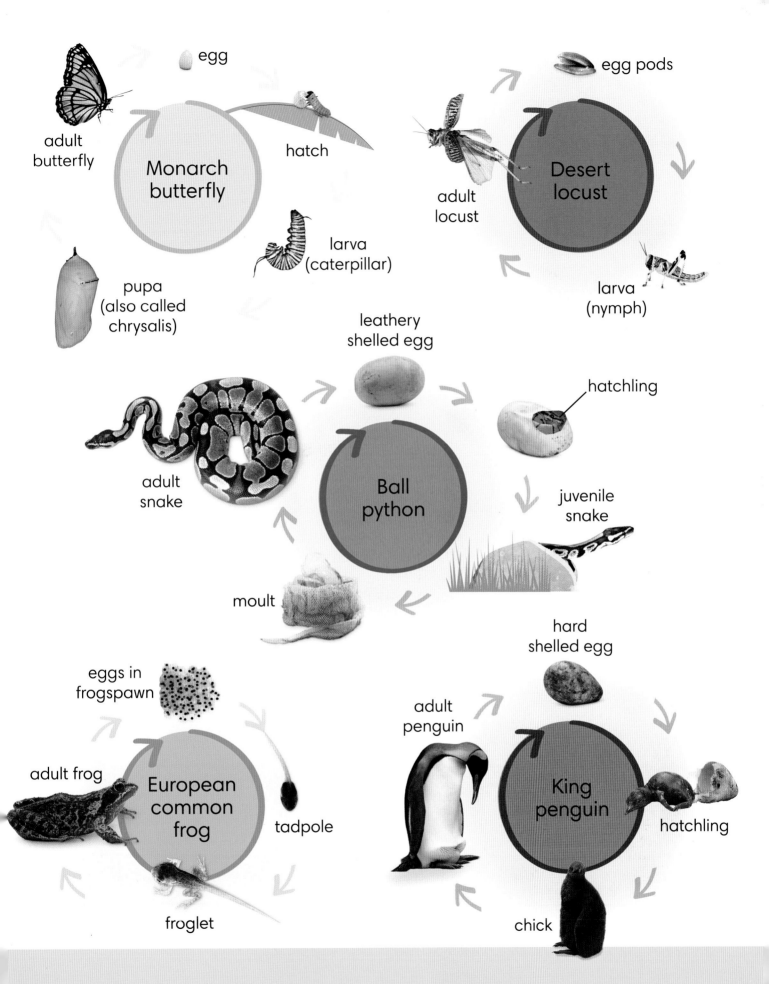

egg

adult
butterfly

Monarch
butterfly

hatch

larva
(caterpillar)

pupa
(also called
chrysalis)

egg pods

Desert
locust

adult
locust

larva
(nymph)

leathery
shelled egg

hatchling

adult
snake

Ball
python

juvenile
snake

moult

hard
shelled egg

eggs in
frogspawn

adult frog

European
common
frog

tadpole

adult
penguin

King
penguin

hatchling

froglet

chick

Do you know where frogs lay their frogspawn?

Animal families

Can you name the female, male, and baby in each of these animal families? Some have special names and others don't.

mare

stallion

bull

foal

cow

calf

boar

cockerel

ewe

ram

lambs

sow

piglet

hen

chicks

male ladybird

tom

bitch

cat

female ladybird

larvae

kitten

puppy

dog

drake

male spider

female spider

duck

duckling

spiderlings

buck or boomer

doe or flyer

joey

doe

stag

boar

man

woman

fawn

sow   cub

male turtle

female turtle

baby

hatchling

Animal groups

What names for groups of animals do you know?

pride of lions

pod of dolphins

flock of sheep

colony of ants

Heads, bodies, and feet

Think of an animal. Imagine its head, body, and feet. Are they the same as yours?

Heads

Which animal has the biggest ears?

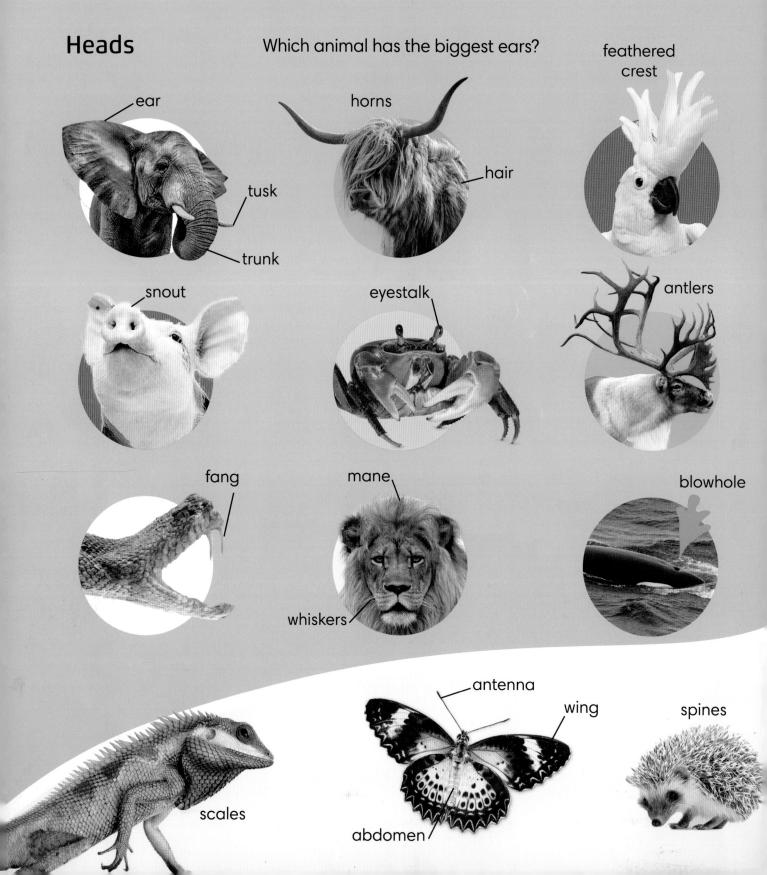

ear

tusk

trunk

horns

hair

feathered crest

snout

eyestalk

antlers

fang

mane

whiskers

blowhole

antenna

wing

spines

scales

abdomen

Feet (and hands!)

tube feet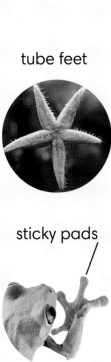

flipper

paws

talons

hooves

sticky pads

prolegs

webbed feet

claws

fin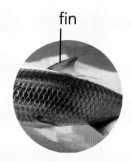

fingers

toes

Why do waterbirds have webbed feet?

skin

Bodies

four-legged

shell

fur

tail

bristles

feathers

exoskeleton
(outside skeleton)

endoskeleton
(inside skeleton)

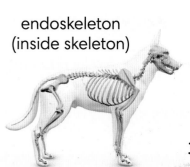

Feeding time

What do animals feed on and how do they eat? Let's take a look.

omnivore
(plant and meat eater)

bears

carnivore
(meat eater)

herbivore
(plant eater)

predator   cheetah

vulture

antelope

graze

scavenger
(eater of
leftovers)

prey

grass

Food chain

          flow of nutrients

All about eating

mouth

Beavers eat
leaves, twigs,
and bark.
They cut
wood to
make dams.

bite and
chew

gnaw

proboscis
(straw-like
mouthpart)

Trap-jaw
ants eat
other
insects.

nectar

mandibles
(mouthparts)

suck

lap

ready to snap

Animals with specialised diets

dung beetle

dung

panda

bamboo

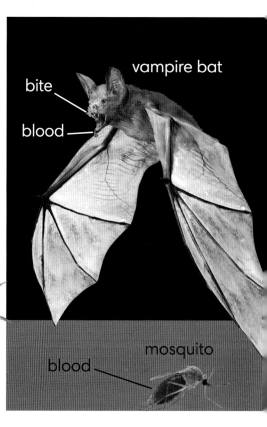

vampire bat

bite

blood

blood

mosquito

Can you name another baby animal that feeds on its mother's milk?

beak

crack!

nut

crush

milk

suckle

whale baleen (filtering mouthparts)

krill

filter feeder (strains food)

Many spiders liquefy the insides of insects, then they suck up the liquid.

liquefy

Communicating

Zoologists can't talk to animals, but they can understand some of their messages. Can you?

Communicating over long distances

low-pitched sound

birdsong

Marking territory

scent marking

posture

hair on end

rearing up

Showing fear or strength

alarm call

Communicating danger

growling

warning of attack

thumping

howling

Communicating "I'm here"

Showing friendship

grooming

cheep cheep

call

Showing where food is

Ants leave a scent trail.

Bees waggle dance (to tell other bees where there are flowers).

Communicating with humans

Koko the gorilla

sign language

Communicating "let's play!"

play bow

A male bird of paradise puts on a display.

A male cricket chirps.

Attracting a mate

Many male birds sing to impress a mate. Some female birds sing, too.

A male pufferfish creates a nest ready for a female's eggs.

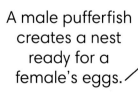

Which animal wags its tail to show different emotions?

wolves

Animal comparisons

Big or small, wild or tame, venomous or harmless – just look at all these animal differences!

tame

cat

fastest on land

cheetah

two of the slowest

snail

sea anemone

What is the biggest animal that walks on land? (Clue: it has a long trunk.)

domesticated

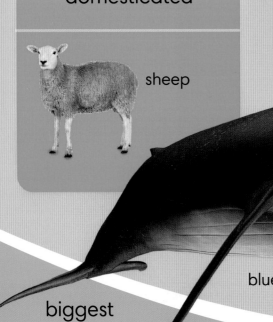

sheep

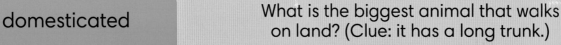

smallest living things

blue whale

heavy

light

biggest

microorganisms

solitary

snow leopard

social

dogs

diurnal
(active in the daytime)

butterfly

venomous

viper

harmless

slowworm

eye-catching

camouflaged

bird of paradise

octopus

nocturnal
(active at night)

moth

tall

giraffe

short

mouse

plain

horse

patterned

zebra

tiger

fox

omnivore

carnivore

herbivore

rabbit

Poo

Poo comes in many shapes and sizes!

Which animal has cube-shaped poo?

rabbit droppings

fox poo

bird dropping
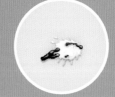

lizard poo

wombat poo

Animal clues

Learn to recognise the poo of different animals. Look out for rotting plants, too – these are being eaten by animals and microbes. You might also find evidence of things that lived long ago.

Rotting plants

What creatures are eating the log?

microbes

More animal clues

shark teeth

shells

skeleton

bones

animal tracks

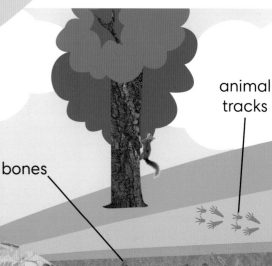

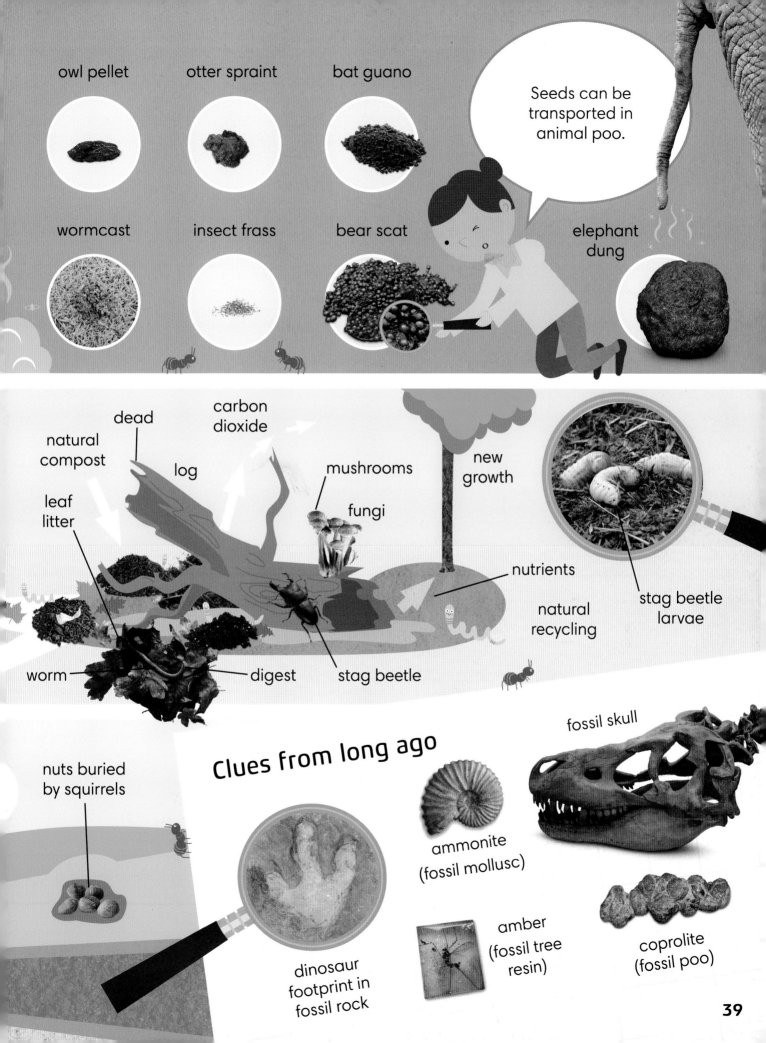

owl pellet

otter spraint

bat guano

Seeds can be transported in animal poo.

wormcast

insect frass

bear scat

elephant dung

natural compost

dead

carbon dioxide

log

mushrooms

fungi

new growth

leaf litter

nutrients

stag beetle larvae

natural recycling

worm

digest

stag beetle

nuts buried by squirrels

Clues from long ago

fossil skull

ammonite (fossil mollusc)

dinosaur footprint in fossil rock

amber (fossil tree resin)

coprolite (fossil poo)

Gardens and parks

There are lots of wonderful things to see and do in a garden or park.

bushes

pond

frog

squirrel

bee

pollinator

apple blossom

spider

spider's web

bird feeder

water butt

shed

rake

flowerpots

hose

sparrow

watering can

bird table

grasshopper

All insects have six legs. Are woodlice crustaceans or insects?

ant

woodlouse

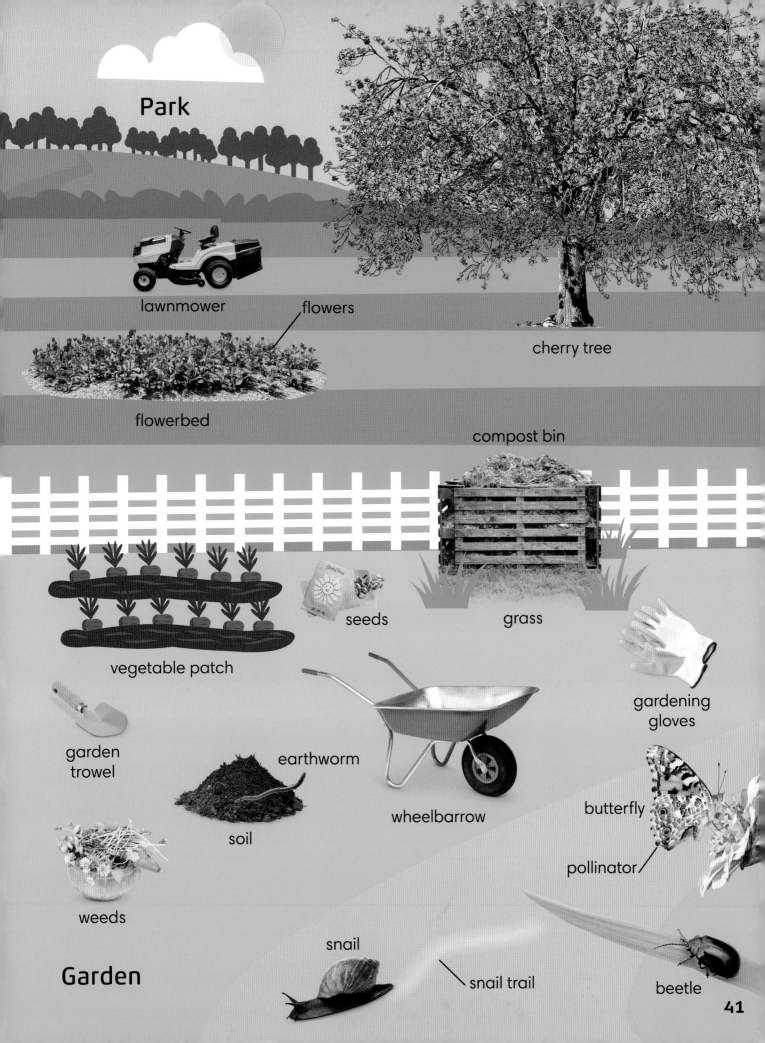

Park

lawnmower

flowers

cherry tree

flowerbed

compost bin

seeds

grass

vegetable patch

gardening gloves

garden trowel

earthworm

soil

wheelbarrow

butterfly

pollinator

weeds

snail

snail trail

beetle

Garden

41

Fields and meadows

Some fields are planted with crops. Others are full of wildflowers. Grassland can be green and grassy or dusty and dry.

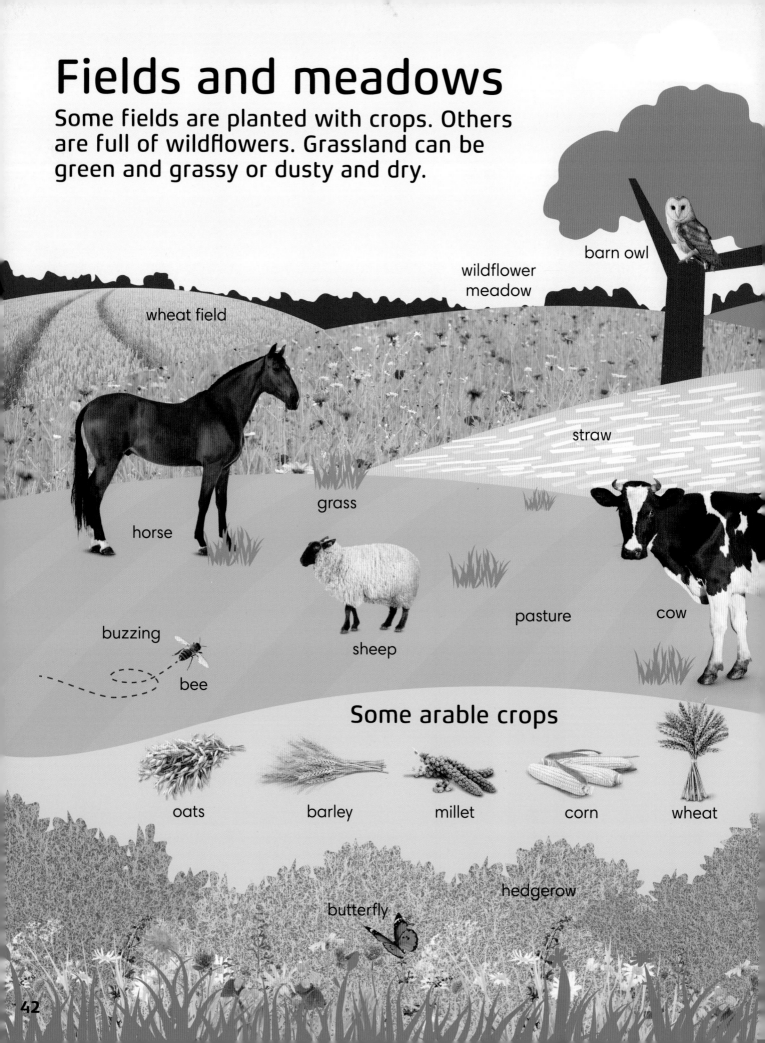

barn owl

wildflower meadow

wheat field

straw

grass

horse

buzzing

bee

sheep

pasture

cow

Some arable crops

oats

barley

millet

corn

wheat

hedgerow

butterfly

Can you think of a food
you like that contains
an arable crop?

osprey

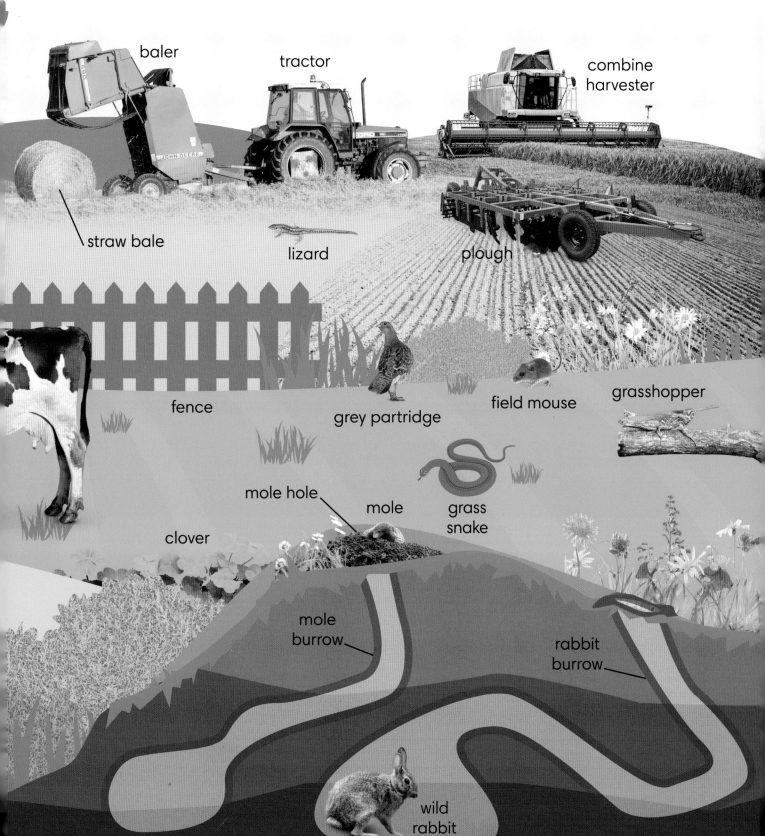

baler

tractor

combine
harvester

straw bale

lizard

plough

fence

grey partridge

field mouse

grasshopper

mole hole

mole

grass
snake

clover

mole
burrow

rabbit
burrow

wild
rabbit

43

Woodlands

Animals find plenty to eat in woodlands, and protection from the worst of the weather.

horse chestnut leaf

conker shell

conker

chirping

chiffchaff

red squirrel

hooting

tawny owl

bird's nest

undergrowth

bluebells

horse chestnut tree

rustling

fawn

ferns

dragonfly

pond

pond snail

pond skater

fox

rhinoceros beetle

fox den

European forest

Can you spot a baby deer?

American redwood forest

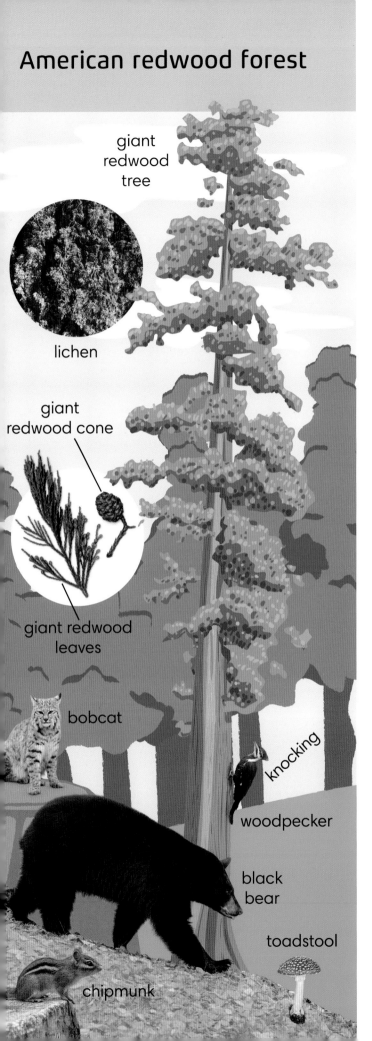

giant redwood tree

lichen

giant redwood cone

giant redwood leaves

bobcat

knocking

woodpecker

black bear

toadstool

chipmunk

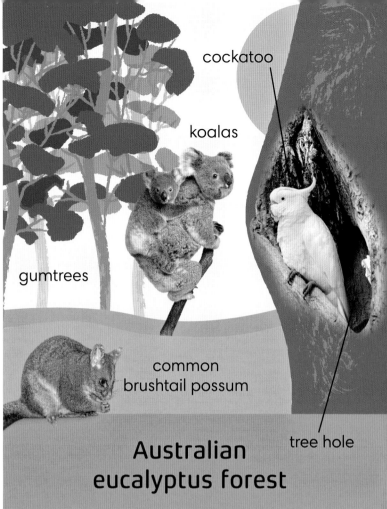

cockatoo

koalas

gumtrees

common brushtail possum

tree hole

Australian eucalyptus forest

bamboo

plum blossom

panda

Chinese bamboo forest

Rivers

Animals live in rivers, on riverbanks, and on the flat areas next to rivers, called floodplains.

weeping willow tree

burrow

riverbank

muskrat

fishing

water vole

Canada goose

osprey

fresh water

salmon

moorhen

carp

reeds

mayfly

pondweed

stickleback

crayfish

pike

current

rapids

canoe

wild swimming

swan

Spot the creature in the water that has an exoskeleton (a hard outer skeleton).

duck

heron

dragonfly

otter

beaver

marsh

Where does a river meet the sea?

sea   estuary   river

weir

floodplain

waterfall

Oceans and coasts

Most of Earth's surface is covered with water. That is why it looks blue from space.

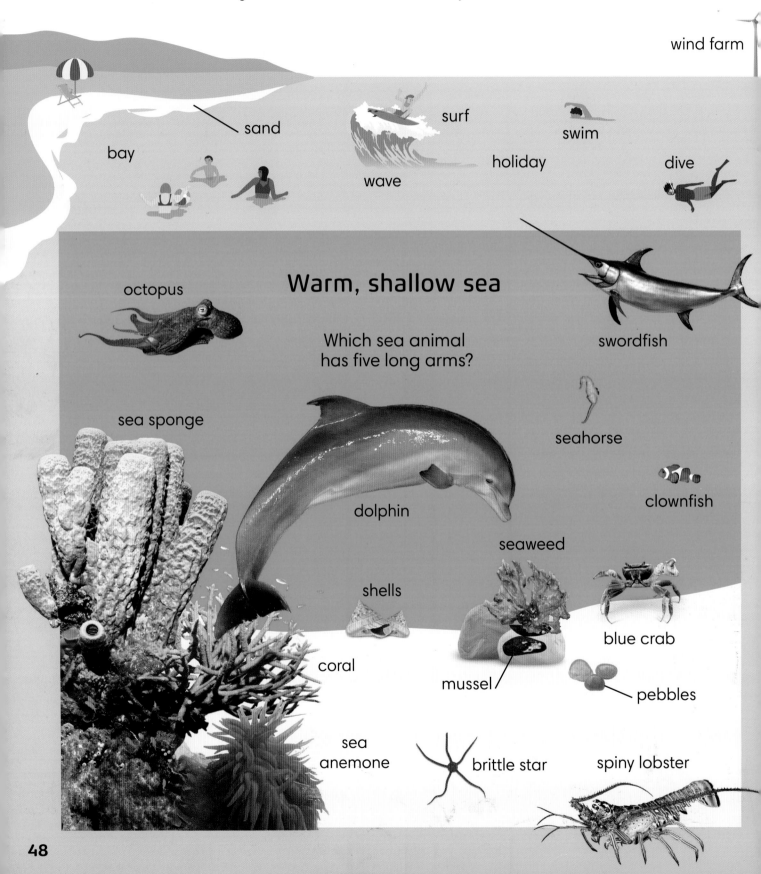

wind farm

sand

surf

swim

bay

holiday

dive

wave

octopus

Warm, shallow sea

swordfish

Which sea animal has five long arms?

sea sponge

seahorse

clownfish

dolphin

seaweed

shells

blue crab

coral

mussel

pebbles

sea anemone

brittle star

spiny lobster

What can you see that produces electricity?

gull

stormy

oil rig

seal

cliffs

fishing boat

shrimp

rockpool

island

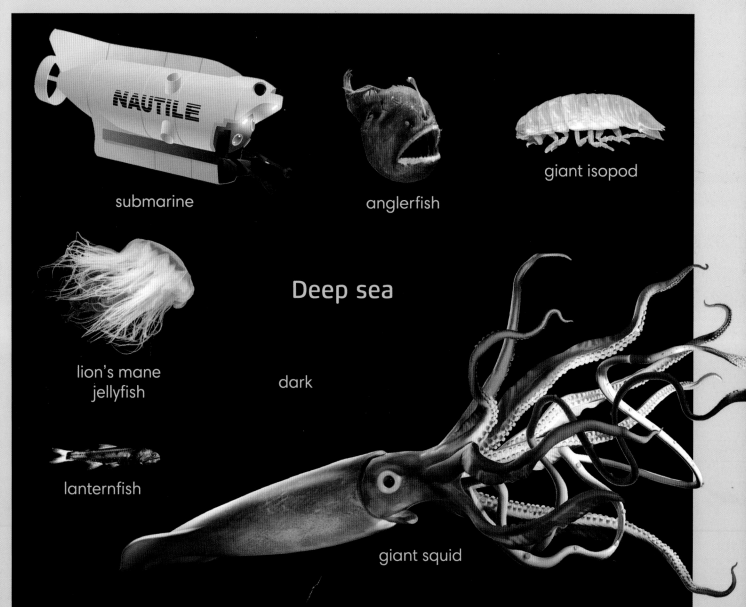

submarine

anglerfish

giant isopod

lion's mane jellyfish

Deep sea

dark

lanternfish

giant squid

Rainforests

Many animal species live in rainforests, and there are lots of new species still to be discovered. Let's look at what lives in the Amazon rainforest of South America.

high

capuchin monkey

climb

sloth

hang

sunny

kapok tree

howler monkey

Emergent layer

vampire bat

fly

macaw

glide

harpy eagle

tree boa

blue morpho butterfly

toucan

green iguana

What sounds might you hear in a rainforest?

red-eyed
tree frog

damp

bananas

cocoa tree

Canopy

cocoa
pod

jaguar

jewel beetle

orchid bee

orchid

nutrient
rich

fungi

decay

buttress
roots

Understorey

giant
centipede

scorpion

churo snail

Forest floor

armadillo

leaf cutter
ant

harlequin
beetle

giant
anteater

51

Savannahs

Savannahs are flat grasslands with few trees. There are often wildfires, but plants regrow. Some of the biggest savannahs are in Africa, South America, and Australia.

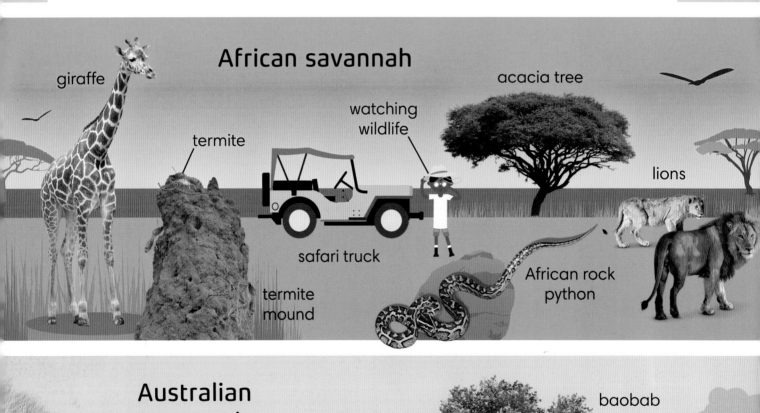

African savannah

giraffe

termite

watching wildlife

acacia tree

lions

termite mound

safari truck

African rock python

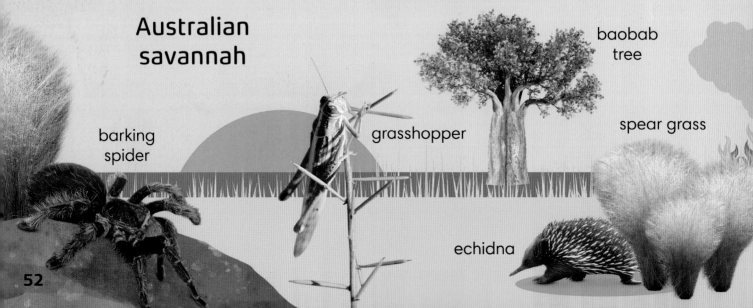

Australian savannah

baobab tree

barking spider

grasshopper

spear grass

echidna

South American savannah

pampas grass

rhea

guinea pig

pampas fox

puma

footprints

Which big mammal has a very long nose?

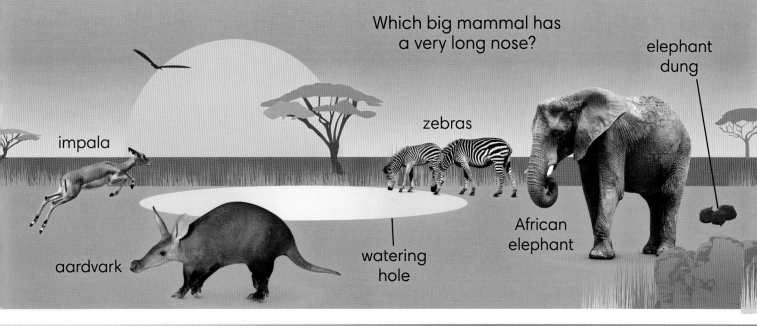

elephant dung

impala

zebras

aardvark

watering hole

African elephant

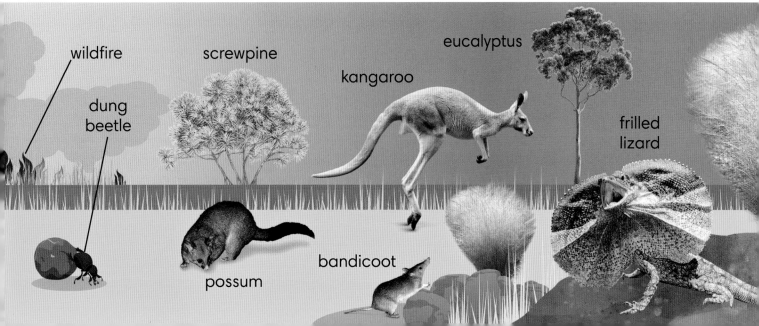

wildfire

screwpine

eucalyptus

dung beetle

kangaroo

frilled lizard

possum

bandicoot

Deserts

Deserts can be hot or cold, but they all get very little rain. Let's look around the Chihuahuan Desert in Mexico.

red-tailed hawk

hunt

Food chain

hiss

rattle

rattlesnake

flow of nutrients

jackrabbit

prickly pear cactus

What eats what in the food chain?

lizard

tumbleweed

coyote

desert kit fox

barrel cactus

dry

jaguar

golden eagle

sand dune

hot

sun

arid

grasshopper

dust storm

scorpion

bighorn sheep

sand

saguaro cactus

Find three birds and two reptiles.

Joshua tree

roadrunner

bobcat

red-spotted toad

yucca   aloe

desert ants

shade

tarantula

Mountains

Mountains are towering lands of earth and stone. It gets colder as you go higher, so mountains are often snowy at the top.

golden eagle

snow

cold

pine marten

hiking

sky

mountain goat

stone

foothill

hiking boots

lynx

wolf

red squirrel

reindeer

cave

bear cub

Where could the mother bear make her den?

brown bear

cloud

summit

snowflakes

peregrine
falcon

ski
poles

ski

frozen

mountain
climber

rope

skier

mountain

tent

camping

cyclists

bicycle

path

waterfall

monarch
butterflies

marmot

fish

plunge pool

rocks

Arctic and Antarctic

Some amazing animals and plants have adapted to survive in the freezing polar habitats of the Arctic and the Antarctic.

The wildlife is different in each place. Do penguins live in the Arctic or the Antarctic?

Arctic

Arctic cottongrass

bog bilberry

grayleaf willow

reindeer lichen

snowy owl

walrus

Arctic tern

rocky shoreline

Arctic fox

lemming

reindeer

Arctic hare

polar bear

beluga whale

harp seal

ice

frozen

narwhal

Antarctic

polar lights

Antarctic hair grass

Antarctic pearlwort

peak

mountain

snow

valley

wandering albatross

snow petrel

polar desert

iceberg

orca

adelie penguin

krill

leopard seal

Weddell seal

Spot three Antarctic mammals.

emperor penguin

starfish

gentoo penguin

Protecting nature

We should take care of our world.
The choices we make can harm or
protect nature.

Which of the things
on these pages help
to protect nature?

Our animals

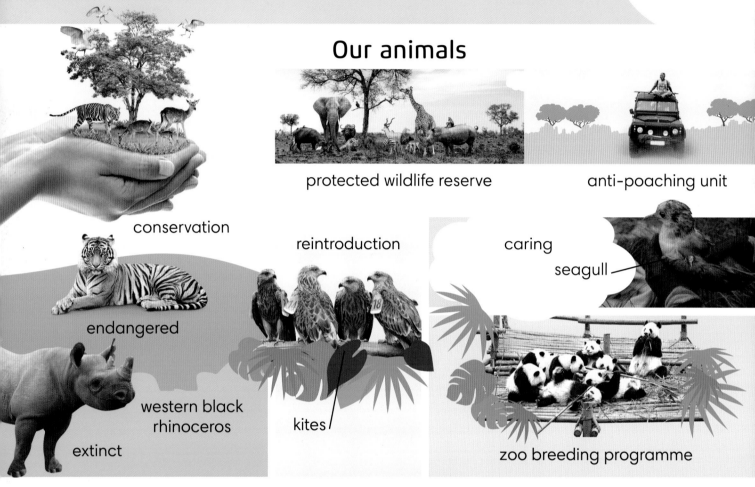

protected wildlife reserve

anti-poaching unit

conservation

reintroduction

caring

seagull

endangered

western black
rhinoceros

kites

extinct

zoo breeding programme

Our farming

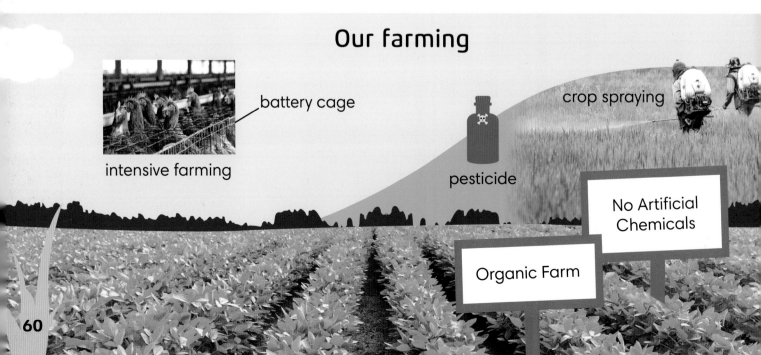

battery cage

crop spraying

intensive farming

pesticide

No Artificial
Chemicals

Organic Farm

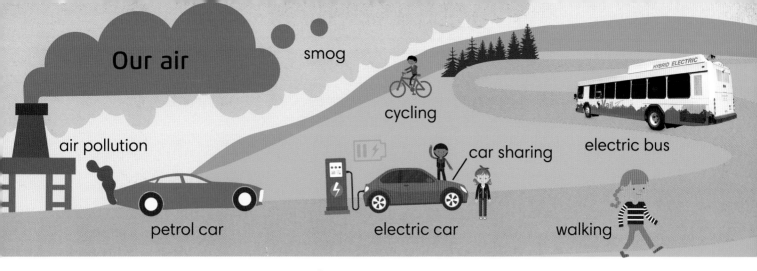

Our air

smog

cycling

air pollution

car sharing

electric bus

petrol car

electric car

walking

Our trees

deforestation

reforestation

Our climate

Can we do something to help nature today?

global warming

wildfires

Our oceans

ocean litter

floods

Reducing
Reusing
Recycling

polar ice caps melting

cleaning up

Working with nature

There are many ways to work with nature, including jobs in which you can help to protect our planet and the species that live on it.

air quality scientist: checks air pollution

farmer

geologist: studies Earth's rocks

forester: looks after forests

zoologist: studies animals

entomologist: studies insects

environmental scientist: studies the environment

botanist: studies plants

gardener

tree surgeon

zookeeper

marine biologist: studies ocean life

vet

environmental activist: supports protecting the environment

natural history museum event manager

ecologist: studies living things and their environment

street cleaner

wildlife author

wildlife photographer

aquarist: manages an aquarium

countryside ranger: looks after the countryside

safari guide

wildlife presenter

environmental engineer: designs things for the environment

animal rescue worker

seismologist: studies earthquakes

Which of these jobs would you like to do?

Acknowledgements

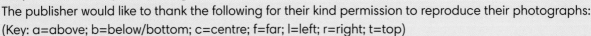

DK would like to thank: Victoria Palastanga and Eleanor Bates for additional design work; Jagtar Singh for additional DTP design work; Adhithi Priya, Sakshi Saluja, Rituraj Singh, Sumedha Chopra, and Vagisha Pushp for additional picture research work; Polly Goodman for proofreading.

The publisher would like to thank the following for their kind permission to reproduce their photographs:

(Key: a=above; b=below/bottom; c=centre; f=far; l=left; r=right; t=top)

1 123RF.com: Liubov Shirokova (clb). **Dreamstime.com:** Marc Bruxelle (cra); Isselee (tc); Vvoevale (tl); Yinan Zhang (cl); Svetlana Larina / Blair_witch (fclb); Nejron (cb); Sabelskaya (br). **2 Dorling Kindersley:** Tom Grey (cla); Natural History Museum, London (tr). **Getty Images / iStock:** photo5963 (clb). **3 123RF.com:** isselee / Eric Isselee (bc); Prapan Ngawkeaw (cb/road); jackf / Iakov Filimonov (bl/wolf). **Dreamstime.com:** Iakov Filimonov (clb/goat); Phartisan (rock x3); Jpsdk / Jens Stolt (butterflies x 3); Yotrak (cb/tent); Jackf / Iakov Filimonov (bc/reindeer); Nelikz (bl/squirrel). **Shutterstock.com:** Aleksandr Pobedimskiy (clb/sandstone). **6–7 Dreamstime.com:** Gritsalak Karalak (c). **6 Dreamstime.com:** Astrofireball (c). **7 Dorling Kindersley:** Dan Crisp (ca); Natural History Museum, London (crb); James Kuether (cb); Jon Hughes (bc). **Dreamstime.com:** Nicolas Fernandez (c); Markus Gann / Magann (tr). **8 123RF.com:** algre (crb). **Dreamstime.com:** Costasz (bc); Tomasz Śmigla (bc/cups); Vchalup (br); Rui Matos / Rolmat (cra); Rob Wilson / Robwilson39 (cr). **9 123RF.com:** julynx (tl); Martin Spurny (cla); Natthawut Panyosaeng / aopsan (ca). **Alamy Stock Photo:** Mouse in the House (bl). **Dreamstime.com:** Sergey Dzyuba (cr); Elena Kazanskaya (cla/bin); Tele52 (cra); Radha Karuppannan / Radhuvenki (clb/x2); Stockphototrends (bc). **Getty Images / iStock:** DigitalVision Vectors / bubaone (cl); photo5963 (c); youngID (ftl); pterwort (br). **10 123RF.com:** Inna Astakhova (crb); tempusfugit (bc); nerthuz (cb). **Dorling Kindersley:** Tracy Morgan (cb/dog). **Dreamstime.com:** Melanie Hobson (ca/landscape); Nexus7 (t); Isselee (cl); Theo Malings (clb); Eric Isselee (cr). **11 123RF.com:** Aaron Amat (clb/x3); Dmitry Rukhlenko / dimol (fcra). **Alamy Stock Photo:** Justin Kase z12z (fbl). **Dreamstime.com:** Billy Ber (tr); Narathip Ruksa / Narathip12 (ftr); Cammeraydave (cb); Cynoclub (bc); Jeroen Van Den Broek / Vandenbroek29 (bc/GuideDog); PhotoChur (br); Zbynek Burival / Merial (fbr). **Fotolia:** Eric Isselee (bl); Norman Pogson (ca). **Getty Images / iStock:** Mac99 (cra); pifate (crb). **12 123RF.com:** fireflamenco (x3). **Dreamstime.com:** Catalin205 (clb, crb); Vectorikart (cra); Stockoxinoxi (ca); Thomas Holt (cl); Macrovector (clb/net); Photka (br). **13 Dreamstime.com:** Akinshin (tr); Vectorikart (cla); Andreanita (tr/bear); Miramisska (cra); Pavel Rodimov (c/stargazing); Kotenko (c); Gerald Zaffuts (c/storytelling); Christinlola (cr); Sabelskaya (clb); Kellyrichardsonfl (bl); Pavel Naumov (cb/x4); Sergiy Bykhunenko (br); Macrovector (ca). **14 Dreamstime.com:** Andreiuc88 (cb); Antares614 (c); Nehru (br). **15 123RF.com:** Rune Kristoffersen (cla). **Dreamstime.com:** Mihai Andritoiu (cb); Mishoo (tl); Artisticco Llc (tr). **16 123RF.com:** justoomm (bc); Kitsadakron Pongha (cra); nasaimages (c/cyclone). **Alamy Stock Photo:** Mike Hill (c). **Dreamstime.com:** Arevhamb (bl); Andrey Armyagov (cla); Hulv850627 (cl); Justin Hobson (cr); Trekandshoot (clb); Thescv (cb); Elantsev (crb); Ruthchoi (br). **17 123RF.com:** alicenerr (c). **Alamy Stock Photo:** SPUTNIK (cra). **Dreamstime.com:** Giuseppe Di Paolo (ca); Siempreverde22 (cla); Dmitry Pichugin / Dmitryp (ca/Everest); Valore (cl); Unissunil (c/Mawsynram); Jon Chica Parada (cr). **Getty Images:** Daniel Osterkamp (bc). **Getty Images / iStock:** Jorge Villalba (bl). **18 123RF.com:** Ruth Jenkinson / stevanzz (bl); Andrzej Tokarski / ajt (tc); Przemyslaw Koch (fclb). **Dorling Kindersley:** Liberty's Owl, Raptor and Reptile Centre, Hampshire, UK (crb); Thomas Palmer (cb). **Dreamstime.com:** Digitalimagined (clb/liverwort); Anna Sedneva / Sedneva (clb/grass); Vitalssss (c); Sarah2 (crb/tick); Ildar Galeev (bc). **Fotolia:** Karl Bolf (fcrb). **Getty Images / iStock:** Antagain (clb). **19 123RF.com:** smileus (tc); Pavlo Vakhrushev / vapi (cla); Ten Theeralerttham / rawangtak (cl); Thawat Tanhai (bl). **Dreamstime.com:** Conchasdiver (clb); Lgor Dolgov / Id1974 (tr); Ronniechua (c); Kotomiti_okuma (cb); Kazoka (cr). **20 Dreamstime.com:** Cherdchai Chaivimol (cb/bud); Vaclav Volrab (cla); Kaiwut Niponkaew (ca); Tomboy2290 (cra/Basil); Natali572 (cra); Ppy2010ha (clb); Dewins (bc); Lepas (bl); Oleg Dudko (fbl); Bogdan Lazar (cb); Songyuth Unkong (crb); Mikhail Dudarev (br). **21 123RF.com:** Anna Liebiedieva / utima (cl); olegdudko (c/Kiwi). **Dorling Kindersley:** Neil Fletcher (cra). **Dreamstime.com:** Anton Ignatenco (c); Zerbor (cla); David Ridley (ftl); Paul Rookes (tl); Zerbor (fcla); Natika (clb); Elena Schweitzer / Egal (cb); Roman Ivaschenko (bl); Roman Ivaschenko (bl/seaweed); Vetre Antanaviciute-meskauskiene (bc). **Getty Images / iStock:** DNY59 (fcra). **Shutterstock.com:** Daydreamr Digital Studio (tr). **22 Dorling Kindersley:** Centre for Wildlife Gardening / London Wildlife Trust (ca). **Dreamstime.com:** Marc Bruxelle (cl); Vvoevale (cla); Pipa100 (clb); Dreamstock (cb); Filmfoto (bl); Anatoliy Mandrichenko (bc). **22–23 Dreamstime.com:** Andreykuzmin (b); Zerbor (c). **23 Dreamstime.com:** Denira777 (cra); Anton Ignatenco (tr); Ievgenii Tryfonov (bc); Setory (br); Majormetts (crb); Zorica Vitanovic (ca). **24 Dreamstime.com:** Domnitsky (ca); Md. Rakibul Hassan (sunflower life cycle); Ilonai (tr). **25 Dreamstime.com:** Elena Elisseeva (cr); Nadiia Havryliuk Kharzhevska (bl/mushroom cycle); Luayana (tl/apple tree life cycle); Angelo Gilardelli (tr); Lenazajchikova (crb); Pavel Rodimov (br); Wirestock (clb); Thawats (cla). **26 123RF.com:** Aleksandr Ermolaev (cr). **Dreamstime.com:** Anankkml (bc); Photodeti (ca); Wirestock (br). **Fotolia:** Mark Higgins (fbr). **Getty Images / iStock:** LUNAMARINA (bl). **27 Alamy Stock Photo:** SConcepts (bl). **Dreamstime.com:** Jason W. Baker (tl); Isselee (cra); Svetlana Larina / Blair_witch (ftl); Pimmimemom (tc); Stevenrussellsmithphotos (ca, fcla); Vasiliy Vishnevskiy (cl); Isselee (cr); Cinnamongirl (crb). **Science Photo Library:** Claude Nuridsany & Marie Perennou (tr). **Shutterstock.com:** Lamnoi Manas (cb). **28 123RF.com:** Anna Utekhina (bc). **Dreamstime.com:** Accept001 (c); Isselee (bc/dalmatian); Judith Dzierzawa (br); Alexander Potapov (clb); Isselee (clb/sheep); Alexander Potapov (cra); Isselee (cra/cow); Tristana / Kseniya Abramova (ca); Isselee (cla). **Fotolia:** Anatolii (cb); Olena Pantiukh (crb). **Getty Images:** mikroman6 (bl). **29 123RF.com:** Cathy Keifer (tc); smileus (tr). **Alamy Stock Photo:** Lee Dalton (clb). **Dorling Kindersley:** British Wildlife Centre, Surrey, UK (cla). **Dreamstime.com:** Linda Caldwell (bl); Toby Gibson (bc); Dizzizzmee (ca); Paul Farnfield (fcla); Steve Oehlenschlager (tl); Brett Hondow (tc/wolf spider). **Fotolia:** Eric Isselee (c). **Getty Images:** Photodisc / Don Farrall (ftl). **30 123RF.com:** Visarute Angkatavanich (br). **Dreamstime.com:** Adogslifephoto (cla); Sutisa Kangvansap (bc); Prin Pattawaro (bl); Graeme Snow (crb); Billybruce2000 (cb); Marcin Wojciechowski (cr); Joanna Zopoth Lipiejko (c); Sonsedskaya (cl); Isselee (cra); Gianluca Piccin (ca). **Getty Images / iStock:** RAUSINPHOTO (clb). **31 Dreamstime.com:** Mira Agron (fcl); Sebastian Kaulitzki (br); Pavel Trankov (bc); Steve Allen (bl); Isselee (crb); Isselee (cb); Isselee (clb); Gualberto Becerra (cr); Marco Tomasini (cl); Duncan Noakes (fcra); Wrangel (cra); Melinda Fawver (ca); Svetlana Foote (cla); Dirk Ercken (fcla); Jacoba Susanna Maria Swanepoel (ftr); Wildlife World (tr); Jagodka (tc); Alexandercreator (tl); Reimarg (ftl). **32 123RF.com:** ksena32 / Oksana Tkachuk (cra/chamomile). **Alamy Stock Photo:** Jason Bazzano (br); mauritius images GmbH / Kurt Madersbacher (crb). **Dreamstime.com:** Andreanita (cra); Jose Manuel Gelpi Diaz (cra/vulture); Valentyna Chukhlyebova (ca, cr); Hwongcc (cla, c); Golfxx (cb); Marazem (bc); Dmitry Potashkin (bl); Pop Nukoonrat (sky). **33 Dreamstime.com:** Kharis Agustiar (cr); Jocrebbin (bc); Zedcreations / SACHITH (webs x2); Geerati (cra); Duncan Noakes (cla). **Getty Images:** The Image Bank / Joe McDonald (bl). **Getty Images / iStock:** Parrotstarr (clb); superjoseph (ca); pixhook (ca/bamboo). **34 123RF.com:** Isselee Eric Philippe (c). **Alamy Stock Photo:** Arterra Picture Library / Clement Philippe (br). **Dreamstime.com:** Callipso88 (cr); Vasyl Helevachuk (clb); Dizm (cb); Isselee (crb); Wildlife World (ca); Corey A Ford (cla). **Getty Images:** Photodisc / Don Farrall (bc). **Shutterstock.com:** A.Mac.Photo (cl). **35 123RF.com:** John McAllister (cl); utima (ca). **Alamy Stock Photo:** Bill Coster (c); Pally (br); Les Gibbon (bl). **Dreamstime.com:** Angel Luis Simon Martin (crb); Sergeyoch (clb). **Getty Images:** Hearst Newspapers / San Francisco Chronicle (cra). **Getty Images / iStock:** LuckyTD (tc). **36 123RF.com:** swavo (br); Andrzej Tokarski / ajt (c). **Dorling Kindersley:** Natural History Museum, London (cr). **Dreamstime.com:** Isselee (clb); Alexander Konoplyov (br/bacteria); Stu Porter (cra); Mrrphotography (tl). **Getty Images / iStock:** bbevren (b). **37 123RF.com:** Eric Isselee (crb). Ardea: ar / Science Source / Tom McHugh (cl). **Dorling Kindersley:** Natural History Museum, London (c); Jerry Young (bl); Wildlife Heritage Foundation, Kent, UK (tl). **Dreamstime.com:** Isselee (clb); Jblackstock / Justin Black (cb); Yves Sautter (c/octopus). **38 123RF.com:** Eric Isselee (crb). **Dreamstime.com:** Nchuprin / Andrey Sukhachev (crb/bacteria); Angelique Nijssen (bl); Thatsaphon Saengnarongrat (tr). **38–39 Dreamstime.com:** Andreykuzmin (soil); Smishko (sand texture). **39 123RF.com:** Sayompu Chamnankit (bc/footprints). **Alamy Stock Photo:** Rosanne Tackaberry (br). **Dorling Kindersley. Dreamstime.com:** Andreykuzmin (b); Dijarm (br/graph); Kosmos111 (crb); Сергей Кучугурный (bl); Tamara Kulikova (cb); Hommalai (tc); Dave Nelson (ca); Thanthip Homsansri (cla); Lcrms7 (c); Sripfoto (cl); Typsiaod (clb). **Shutterstock.com:** Mikkola (cr). **40 123RF.com:** alekss / Alexandr Pakhnyushchyy (bl); Anatolii Tsekhmister (cra). **Alamy Stock Photo:** Don Despain (clb). **Dorling Kindersley. Dreamstime.com:** Chernetskaya (fcrb); Uros Petrovic (br); Pzaxe (bc); Loren File (crb); Ivonne Wierink (fcrb/pots); Jgade (cla). **Shutterstock.com:** Artiste2d3d (fcra). **41 Dreamstime.com:** Nikolay Antonov (clb/worm); Kristof Lauwers (br); Pimmimemom (crb); Aleksandr Volkov (clb); Fibobjects (cb); Luceluceluce (clb/soil); Atlasfotoreception (crb/gloves); Boulanger Sandrine (cr); Bundit Minramun (cla); Sergiy1975 (cla/lawn mower). **42–43 Dreamstime.com:** Miriam Doerr (flower x3); Eugenesergeev (grass); Miriam Doerr (wild flowers x3); Supertrooper (c). **42 123RF.com:** peterwaters (clb/bee). **Alamy Stock Photo:** Life on white (cla/horse). **Dorling Kindersley:** Mark Hamblin (cra). **Dreamstime.com:** Animaflora (cb); Tazzymoto (ca); Brett Critchley (cla); Isselee (c); Dzmitry Shpak (fcrb); Inna Kyselova (crb); Nipaporn Panyacharoen (cb/barley); Thawats (bc). **Shutterstock.com:** Volosina (clb). **43 Alamy Stock Photo:** Islandstock (cla). **Dorling Kindersley:** Twan Leenders (cb/snake). **Dreamstime.com:** Tony Bosse (tr); Mickem (bc); Tchara (cb); Chuyu (clb); Sandra Standbridge (crb); Isselee (c); Romica (cra); Palians (cra/harvester); Mariya Kondratyeva (cra/land). **44 123RF.com:** Eric Isselee (c). **Alamy Stock Photo:** Imagebroker / Arco / J. Fieber (bl). **Dorling Kindersley:** Roger Tidman (cl). **Dreamstime.com:** ActiveLines; Macrovector (clb); Isselee (crb); Stephanie Frey (cr); Zerbor (r); Atman (tc); Mille19 (clb/owl). **Getty Images / iStock:** MarkMirror (cb). **45 123RF.com:** Eric Isselee (cra/koala). **Dreamstime.com:** Karen Black (cra); Alexander Potapov (bc); Susan Sheldon (bl); Geoffrey Kuchera (bl/bear); Donyanedomam (clb); Lunamarina (cla); David Steele (ca). **Getty Images / iStock:** GlobalP (cb). **Shutterstock.com:** aphotostory (crb). **46–47 Dreamstime.com:** David Watson (bc). **Shutterstock.com:** xpixel (cane x5). 46 123RF.com: Stanko Mravljak (crb/mayfly). **Dorling Kindersley. Dreamstime.com:** G3miller / Gordon Miller (cr); Zerbor (tr); Eduard Kyslynskyy (ca); Dennis Jacobsen (c); Kevin Wells (cb); Photophreak (crb); Roman Ivaschenko (bl). **Shutterstock.com:** Igor Podgorny (cla). **47 123RF.com:** Stefan Holm (clb/dragonfly); NewAge (cl). **Dorling Kindersley:** Roger Tidman (c). **Dreamstime.com:** Natalya Aksenova (ca); Sova004 (br); Ilyas Kalimullin (crb); Kobchaima (cra); Wirestock (tr); Jnjhuz (clb); Zeytun Images (cb). **48–49 Getty Images / iStock:** photo5963 (ca). **48 Alamy Stock Photo:** Doug Perrine (cr); SBS Eclectic Images (cb); Carsten Reisinger (crb); WaterFrame_dpr (clb). **Dorling Kindersley:** Natural History Museum, London (bl); Linda Pitkin (cl). **Dreamstime.com:** Kevin Panizza (fclb); Pipa100 (cb/lettuce); Harvey Stowe (cra). **Fotolia:** uwimages (crb/anemonefish). **49 123RF.com:** feathercollector (cr). **Alamy Stock Photo:** Minden Pictures / Norbert Wu (c). **Dorling Kindersley:** Tom Grey (tc). **Dreamstime.com:** Robertlasalle (clb). **naturepl.com:** Solvin Zankl (clb/lanternfish). **50–51 Dreamstime.com:** Surachet Khamsuk. **50 123RF.com:** Hal Brindley (tc); Hal Brindley (fcra). **Alamy Stock Photo:** Ivan Kuzmin (tr); Nature Picture Library / MYN / Andrew Snyder (crb); Nature Picture Library / Nick Garbutt (cb/eagle). **Dreamstime.com:** Carlosphotos (bc); Nejron (cb); Chansom Pantip (ftr); Arindam Ghosh (cra). **naturepl.com:** Luiz Claudio Marigo (cla). **51 123RF.com:** anankkml / Anan Kaewkhammul (cb/jaguar); Ajay Bhaskar (r). **Alamy Stock Photo:** Zizza Gordon Insect collection (bl). **Dreamstime.com:** Beautifulblossom (tr); Ryszard Laskowski (bc); Gan Chaonan (br); Whiskybottle (bc/orchid); Isselee (crb); Olga Soe (red flowers x3); Thenatureguy1 (clb); Morley Read (crb/scorpion); Vlad Ivantcov (c); Superoke (cla); Douglas Delgado (cra); Ekays (tl); Waraphot Wapakphet (tl/leaves). **naturepl.com:** Gabriel Rojo (cb). **52 123RF.com:** waldemarus (bc/baobab). **Dreamstime.com:** Bennymarty (crb); Yinan Zhang (cl); Snehitdesign (c); Alexander Shalamov (cr); Kewuwu (c/tree); Fritz Hiersche (bc); Svetlana485 (br); Alexandr Yurtchenko (tc). **naturepl.com:** Piotr Naskrecki (clb/ant 1, clb/ant 2, clb/ant 3). **53 Alamy Stock Photo:** Ken Griffiths (br). **Dorling Kindersley:** Blackpool Zoo (clb); Wildlife Heritage Foundation, Kent, UK (cra). **Dreamstime.com:** Anekoho (cr); Lev Kropotov (crb); Pokec / Jan PokornÃ (cb); Birdiegal717 (bc); Izanbar (bc/possum); Godruma (bl); Johan63 / Johannes Gerhardus Swanepoel (cl); Luca Santilli (c); Vicspacewalker (cla); Luciano Queiroz (ca); Rafael Cerqueira (cla/guinea pig). **54 123RF.com:** cookelma / Andrey Armyagov (b); Anan Kaewkhammul / anankkml (br). **Alamy Stock Photo:** George Brice (bl); Robert Shantz (cb); Mike Lane (cra). **Dorling Kindersley:** Andy and Gill Swash (cr). **Dreamstime.com:** Steve Byland (tl); Derrick Neill (clb); Eutoch (fcr); Eutoch (fcra); Isselee (cla). **55 123RF.**com: alhovik (fcra); Natalie Ruffing (cr); sladerer / Scott Laderer (ca); Ufuk Zivana (ca/cactus). **Alamy Stock Photo:** Arterra Picture Library / Clement Philippe (bc); Nature Picture Library / John Abbott (bl); Rick & Nora Bowers (crb). **Dreamstime.com:** Dfikar (clb); Frank Fichtmueller (fcrb); Skynetphoto (cra); Domnitsky (c); Withgod / Alexander Podshivalov (tl); Vally (cla). **56–56 Dreamstime.com:** Phartisan (rock x4). **56–57 Shutterstock.com:** Aleksandr Pobedimskiy (br/sandstone x2). **56 123RF.com:** jackf / Iakov Filimonov (cb). **Alamy Stock Photo:** Niebrugge Images (br); Paulette Sinclair (cb/bear); Ronald S Phillips (bc). **Dreamstime.com:** Jim Cumming (cra); Jackf / Iakov Filimonov (crb); Iakov Filimonov (ca); Nelikz (clb). **57 123RF.com:** isselee / Eric Isselee (clb); Prapan Ngawkeaw (cl). **Dreamstime.com:** Jpsdk / Jens Stolt (butterflies x3); Yotrak (cla). **Shutterstock.com:** Yes058 Montree Nanta (br/granite). **58 Alamy Stock Photo:** All Canada Photos / Wayne Lynch (fclb); Dembinsky Photo Associates / Alamy / Dominique Braud (cb); Bob Gibbons (cra); Realimage (cla). **Dorling Kindersley:** Jerry Young (crb). **Dreamstime.com:** Devon Crosby (bl); Planetfelicity (br); Luna Vandoorne Vallejo (bc); Grafner (b); Outdoorsman (fcrb); Uhg1234 (clb/reindeer); Zanskar / Vladimir Melnik (cla/walrus); Luis Leamus (cr); Il`mar Idiyatullin (fcra); Troyka (ca). **Getty Images / iStock:** Karyn Schiller (fcla). **59 Alamy Stock Photo:** era-images / Colin Harris (tr); Minden Pictures / Norbert Wu (bc). **Dreamstime.com:** Agami Photo Agency (cla); Photographerlondon (br); Sharon Jones (crb); Vika Ivanets (cb); Freezingpictures / Jan Martin Will (cr); Slowmotiongli (c); Staphy (ca); Biletskiy (t); Viktoria Ivanets (tc). **Getty Images:** Digital Vision / David Tipling (bl). **60 Alamy Stock Photo:** Roger Hutchings (cra); WhiskeyWolf (cl); Ann and Steve Toon (c). **Dreamstime.com:** Adogslifephoto (ca); Chuchart Duangdaw (crb); Biletskiy (b); Comzeal (clb); Hel080808 (cr); Nilanjan Bhattacharya (cla/tiger); Maxirf (cra/anti poaching unit); Sarayut Thaneerat (cla). **61 Dreamstime.com:** Steve Allen (bc); Skylightpictures (cb); Andrey Koturanov (cb/Waterflood); David Pereiras Villagra (br); Romolo Tavani (crb); Win Nondakowit (bl); Gpgroup (clb); Sjors737 (cra); Piotr Wawrzyniuk (cla); Noamfein (tr). **64 Dreamstime.com:** Marc Bruxelle (tr/Maple); Vvoevale (tr); Nadiia Havryliuk Kharzhevska (crb); Zerbor (tr/maple tree)

Cover images: *Front and Back:* **Dreamstime.com:** Irinav; *Front:* **123RF.com:** Aaron Amat bc/ (Ostrich), jackf / Iakov Filimonov cl, madllen (sprout), Liubov Shirokova (Flower), Andrzej Tokarski / ajt fbr, Anatolii Tsekhmister (squirrel); **Dorling Kindersley:** Blackpool Zoo cla, Centre for Wildlife Gardening / London Wildlife Trust (Hollyleaf), Mark Hamblin tc, Liberty's Owl, Raptor and Reptile Centre, Hampshire, UK (tarantula), Natural History Museum, London (butterfly), Jerry Young (Bumblebee); **Dreamstime.com:** Atman (leaf), Marc Bruxelle (MapleLeaf), Carlosphotos (Butterflyx2), Denira777 cr, Lgor Dolgov / Id1974 cra, Dreamstock (Fir), Dvrcan cra/ (weevil), Iakov Filimonov cla/ (goat), Angelo Gilardelli br, Godruma ca/ (beetle), Vasyl Helevachuk (robin), Eric Isselée (Silkworm), Isselee (Deer), Jblackstock / Justin Black tr, Jgade (frog), Johan63 / Johannes Gerhardus Swanepoel (impala), Svetlana Larina / Blair_witch clb, Nejron (parrot), Matee Nuserm fcrb, Pokec / Jan PokornÃ clb/ (Kangaroo), Stu Porter (Cheetah), Alexander Potapov (agaric), Stevenrussellsmithphotos tc/ (Butterfly), Ievgenii Tryfonov cl/ (trunk), Vasiliy Vishnevskiy cb/ (Rook), Vvoevale (brown leaf); **Getty Images:** Fuse cb/ (Jaguar); **Getty Images / iStock:** GlobalP tl, igorkov (eagle); *Back:* **123RF.com:** madllen (sprout), Liubov Shirokova (Flower), Anatolii Tsekhmister (squirrel); **Dorling Kindersley:** Jerry Young (stickleback fish), Centre for Wildlife Gardening / London Wildlife Trust (Hollyleaf), Twan Leenders tl, Liberty's Owl, Raptor and Reptile Centre, Hampshire, UK (tarantula), Natural History Museum, London (butterfly), Jerry Young (Bumblebee); **Dreamstime.com:** Atman (leaf), Marc Bruxelle (MapleLeaf), Dreamstock (Fir), Dvrcan (weevil), Freezingpictures / Jan Martin Will (penguin), Vasyl Helevachuk (robin), Eric Isselée (Silkworm), Isselee (Deer), Jgade (frog), Johan63 / Johannes Gerhardus Swanepoel (impala), Svetlana Larina / Blair_witch ca, Luis Leamus cr, Nejron (parrot), Uros Petrovic crb, Stu Porter (Cheetah), Ievgenii Tryfonov (trunk), Vasiliy Vishnevskiy (Rook), Vvoevale (brown leaf), Zerbor bc; **Getty Images / iStock:** GlobalP (panda), igorkov (eagle); *Spine:* **Dreamstime.com:** Macrovector (snail), Alexander Potapov (agaric)

For further information see: www.dkimages.com